Yellow Umbrella Books are published by Capstone Press
151 Good Counsel Drive, P.O. Box 669, Mankato, Minnesota 56002
http://www.capstone-press.com

Library of Congress Cataloging-in-Publication Data
Curry, Don L.
  What hatches?/by Don L. Curry.
  p. cm.
  Includes index.
  ISBN 0-7368-0721-7
  1. Embryology—Juvenile literature. 2. Eggs—Juvenile literature. [1. Eggs. 2. Animals.]
I. Title.
QL956.5 .C87 2001
591.4'68—dc21   00-036518

Summary: Describes different types of eggs and which animals hatch from them,
including birds, butterflies, frogs, alligators, and fish.

Editorial Credits:
Susan Evento, Managing Editor/Product Development; Elizabeth Jaffe, Senior Editor;
  Charles Hunt, Designer; Kimberly Danger and Heidi Schoof, Photo Researchers

Photo Credits:
Cover: Llewellyn/Pictor; Title Page: Pictor ((top left), Photri-Microstock (bottom left), Photo
Network/Karen Lawrence (top right), David M. Dennis/TOM STACK & ASSOCIATES (bottom
right); Page 2: A. Morris/Pictor; Page 3: Visuals Unlimited/Dick Poe; Page 4: (top to bottom
right) Visuals Unlimited/Dick Poe, Visuals Unlimited/S. Maslowski, Unicorn Stock Photos/Ron
Holt, Robert McCaw; Page 5: Inga Spence/TOM STACK & ASSOCIATES; Page 6: Visuals
Unlimited/Richard Carlton, Photri-Microstock (inset); Page 7: David M. Dennis/TOM STACK &
ASSOCIATES; Page 8: John Shaw/TOM STACK & ASSOCIATES (top left), Visuals
Unlimited/Robert W. Domm (top right), David M. Dennis/TOM STACK & ASSOCIATES (bot-
tom left and right); Page 9: Visuals Unlimited/K.B. Sandved; Page 10: Joe McDonald/TOM
STACK & ASSOCIATES; Page 11: Tess & David Young/TOM STACK & ASSOCIATES; Page 12:
Photri-Microstock/Charles Philip, David M. Dennis/TOM STACK & ASSOCIATES (inset); Page
13: Jeffrey Rich/Pictor; Page 14: Thomas Kitchin/TOM STACK & ASSOCIATES (top left),
Visuals Unlimited/Steve McCutcheon (top right), Jeffrey Rich/Pictor (bottom left), Jeff
Foott/TOM STACK & ASSOCIATES (bottom right); Page 15: Visuals Unlimited/Dick Poe (top
left), Inga Spence/TOM STACK & ASSOCIATES (top right), David M. Dennis/TOM STACK &
ASSOCIATES (middle left), Visuals Unlimited/K.B. Sandved (middle right), Tess & David
Young/TOM STACK & ASSOCIATES (bottom left), Jeffrey Rich/Pictor (bottom right); Page 16:
Robert McCaw (top left), Visuals Unlimited/Richard L. Carlton (top right), Visuals
Unlimited/Robert W. Domm (middle left), Joe McDonald/TOM STACK & ASSOCIATES (mid-
dle right), Photri-Microstock/Charles Philip (bottom left), Thomas Kitchin/TOM STACK &

1 2 3 4 5 6 06 05 04 03 02 01

What Hatches?

by Don L. Curry

Consulting Editor: Gail Saunders-Smith, Ph.D.
Consultants: Claudine Jellison and Patricia Williams,
Reading Recovery Teachers
Content Consultant: Rafe M. Brown, Research Associate,
Texas Memorial Museum, University of Texas at Austin

Yellow Umbrella Books

an imprint of Capstone Press
Mankato, Minnesota

What hatches?
Baby birds hatch from eggs.
Many other animals hatch
from eggs too.
Their eggs all look different.

Look at this egg.

The mother lays her eggs
on a leaf.
When they hatch, the babies eat
their egg covering and then
they eat the leaf.
What will hatch from this egg?

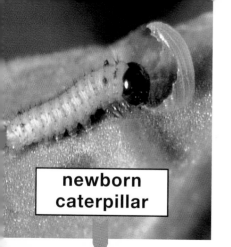

newborn caterpillar

A caterpillar will hatch. It will eat and grow. It changes into a chrysalis. It becomes a butterfly.

caterpillar

chrysalis

butterfly

4

Look at these eggs.

They are the largest eggs laid
by any animal alive today.
Each egg weighs about 3 pounds
(1.4 kilograms).
What will hatch from these eggs?

Ostriches will hatch.
The ostrich is the largest bird
alive today. It can grow to be
7 feet (2.1 meters) tall.
It can run 40 miles
(64 kilometers) an hour!

Look at these eggs.
The mother lays her eggs
in ponds and swamps.
These eggs like warm water.

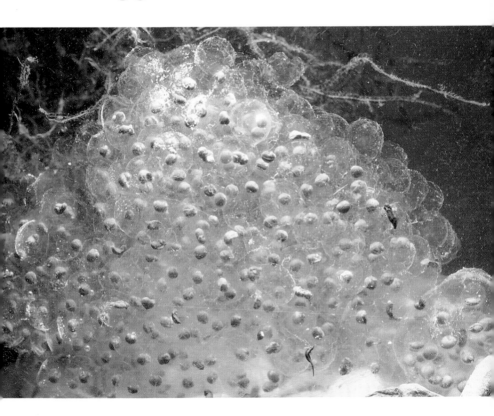

What will hatch from these eggs?

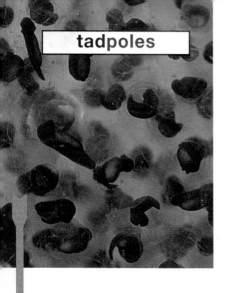
tadpoles

frog

Tadpoles will hatch.

Tadpoles eat and change.

Tadpoles grow to be frogs.

Frogs live on land and in water.

growing tadpole

young frog

Look at this egg.
The mother lays her egg
on rocks.
Then she goes off to eat.
The father keeps the egg warm
by carrying it on his feet.

What will hatch from this egg?

A penguin
will hatch.
Penguins live
in cold
and windy
places.
The father
penguin
keeps the
young
penguin
warm
and safe.

Look at these eggs.
The mother lays her eggs
on the edge of a swamp.
They will look like their mother
when they are born.

What will hatch from these eggs?

Alligators will hatch.

Alligators live in warm weather
near swamps.

They eat birds, fish,
and even other alligators!

Look at these eggs.
The mother swims upstream
to lay her eggs in the same place
where she was hatched.
She lays hundreds of eggs
at one time.

What will hatch from these eggs?

Salmon will hatch.
The mother lays the eggs
in the rocks along the bottom
of creeks and streams.
Salmon then hatch and swim
back downstream.

eggs

eggs hatching

14

Look at these eggs again.
What will hatch from each egg?

Match what hatched.

Words to Know/Index

Word Count: 350
Early-Intervention Levels: 13–16